Platinum Poetry Series

Lyrics

William Driscoll

Terracom Books

Lyrics
Terracom Books Platinum Poetry Series/January 2014
First Edition

Published by Terracom Books
A Division of Terracom Media

ISBN–13: 978–0–615–95516–2

Terracom Media

mediaterracom@gmail.com
wb

CONTENTS

Five Eggs in Springtime

When the wind blows warm from the south
heavy with the scent of loam and pine
the forest behind the old shed
shudders, cracks under the weight
of wet snow in spring and expectation
I close my eyes to taste the bloom
of springs before, that came and to
the lover, poet, fool conjured immortality

Did Whitman, in the freezing blood of young
boys dying with winter on some distant field,
taste such sorrow? And sing?
Did Arnold bear such melancholy by his moon-
blanched shore and choose to love?

Human misery is less inspiring amid the maple
and pine when springtime brings the scent of death

Across the holt a neighbor's clearing trees
rough men balance chainsaws with their bellies
and callused hands or ride high upon
smoking machines with claws and teeth chewing
up the pines, seeing only wood and worse

As some foreign army in a distant field they fall
in uniforms of needles and dried brown leaves

one by one shake the earth and tremble down
they were here before the roads and houses
(the difference and degrees) where soft malice
warms its hands like a Bedouin before a desert fire
they were here before the fall

When I stalked those woods in spring, peered
in its hollow stumps, kicked its rotted logs
saw dead raccoons with black and crawling eyes
and flightless birds bent like broken sticks, drunk
on despair and the liveliness of death and spring

When under a leaning birch, I came upon a nest
abandoned on its side and listing
in it five small eggs bleached as the bark above
nestled in a pile of twigs, five small prayers
of peace thrust to the future unrealized
five fragile dreams broken and consumed

Were We Once filled with Sky and Lake

Were we once filled with sky and lake
and covered with mud?
blue as a jay and daring as a crow?
I don't remember
something tells me that we were
in Erin I can see it
all dancing Erin pigtails and promise
can I wear a party dress? she smiles
to climb a tree? I ask exasperated
to climb a tree...

Were we once bright as a star
and open as a field?
sharp as a blade of grass
and green as summer?
we might have been
I seem to recall
in Sean I can see it
all searching Sean eyes and fingers
that's a Cosmos there
that's Queen Ann's Lace
if you say so, so
if you say so, so...

Were we once brown as the earth
and ripe as a berry?

shifting like a humming bird

and soaking like a sponge?

I don't know

it's quite likely we were

in Erik I can see it

all smiling Erik all hands all head

all light blue eyes

I'm wearing stardust for my shirt – see?

if only I could tell you where I'm from

before I forget...

If only you could tell us

The Visitor

When I was three, the visitor came
to my house and led me from
root to trunk, from warm bath
water to March rain, from my mother's
breast, my slatted bed to run to him
as if an old friend

And as I ran free as the sunshine on
green grass, pressed footprints in the earth
callow and whispering as the wind
that plays the birch leaves sideways
in the spring, he smiled at me
bone–white and merciless

When I was thirteen, the visitor came again
holding lanterns of gull–flight and
nimbus clouds, baskets of honey–bread
and wild storms and love, love
and I walked with her a while
as if a trusted guide

And she led me to fields of delight
and fruits of mallow sweetness round
the curve of her urging I caressed
the fullness of that promontory
crashed against the black cliffs

of my desire with mad fury
restless as the currents, somber as the grave

And as I forgot the ocean so too
I forgot the shore
for a time
for a time

When I was nineteen, I sat apart silent
a cracked seawall where thousands of
fireflies had lighted for my delight
where moonlight had become woman
and sea tide bliss and there the visitor
touched the sand before my eyes
with snow and ice, whipped the waves
to a dark brooding cascade of hoarfrost
sweeping that ghastly scene with a ghostly
arm it whispered 'I shall return
to collect my payment'

Then vanished on the winds
leaving me frozen and afraid

When I was thirty–two, the visitor appeared
again – a giant dark and brooding
terrible as the gale, empty as a cavern
reaching a shadow hand inside my chest
it took the fire there and snuffed it

'Now you are truly dead'
it said

And I mourned

And since the visitor
hasn't left me but it sits
beside me always, touching my cells
one by one with numbness
like a game, taking bits of me
at a time like twine, to make a nest
my conifer nest

'Will you soon rock me
in your arms, rock me
for all eternity and never
let me go?' I ask

And the visitor smiles

The Dripping Drops of Rain

'The dripping drops
of rain as tears drop
dripping on my window–
pane as stones that night
when you were there so young
so young in the darkness
by a magnolia tree the black
of your hair darker
than my fears

'I see you through my window–
pane asleep in my bed
a sleep so peaceful – to sleep again
my eyes open my head craning
quickly raising firm small breasts
riding the panting of an unstretched waist
smooth honed to greet
the hollow of your hand

'Don't rustle the fallen willow
leaves! the tulip bulbs are newly
planted not that I care about the
flower garden
I'm afraid what my mother
and father might say

'And so I lay darkly
a love's ache baited by
a young heart's hesitancy
a brow furrowing
for your kisses
my pearl diver lungs bursting
for the surface of your sea

'Don't come too close to
the living room window look! the
bushes are newly trimmed not that
I care about the bushes
I'm afraid what my brothers
and sisters might say

'And so I lay, and the night
passes slowly, impatiently
louder each rock
off my window–pane as stones
that night when I was
there so young so young
in the darkness afraid of my
own longings, afraid to fold
myself into your ever pressing
need

'Come tomorrow night or the next
my love the dawn comes

soon then day then dusk
I'll turn my light on for you then I'll
rock your loins in the threshold of
my fearless kisses

'But tonight the grass is new
mown wet with dew
the soil unmarred by footsteps
not that I care about the lawn
I'm afraid what my friends
and neighbors might say

'And so I lay here
in the dark and you gone
and the night and the rain
falls dripping drops as tears
drop dripping
on my window–pane as stones
that night

'One night lost –
so what, when there
seemed so many...'

The Many Coats

In the ancient days the lover wore
a coat of skin the sun rose
unblemished by haze and smoke and age
yet the lover was the same

Her name no more important than the clover
that catches her eye or the smell of grass
wet with morning dew or the robin that feeds
cicadas to its young their beaks darting
upward orange and open greedy and wide

In the child days the lover wore
a coat of cloth the sun seared
the dew dry and the meadow–
shadows grew with gnats and aphids swirling
yet the lover was the same

Her face no more important than the
meadowlark's song that trills her fancy
echoing freely echoing in the hills
swept with day breezes gentle
and penetrating cool and sweet

In the grown days the lover wore
a coat of silk, the sun blazed brightly
on hats of golden feathers

and rows of sequined gems blinding the eye
and clouding the mind
yet the lover was the same

Her body the world now round and fertile
growing as the grains, rising as the yeast
in her brown bread, fecund as the day lily
whose shape draws in the ambling bumblebee
the river is too broad to cross, the nest
filled with colored thread and bits of cloth
the night has round ample arms

In the waning days the lover wore
a coat of taffeta with padded shoulders
and velvet slippers the sun arced
shadowless beyond the rowan trees
and juniper fermented to cool the day
yet the lover was the same

Her body no more seen now than
the earthworm in its domain
beneath her feet, or the white rose
whose petals fall to soil above its
head, join the parting leaves
to form a grave for summer's promises
and autumn's colorful dances

Again in the ancient days
the lover wore a coat of skin

the sun set red–purple as
the water violet hazed and heavy
as the night sky fulfilled in its course
yet the lover was the same

So will it be with you my love

Death came Anyway

Death came anyway –
how I loved that magnolia tree
I had planted it myself
one Mother's Day when
my mother was young
and its roots dug into
my core, more thoroughly
than a bore, more concretely
than a stonewall
I had planted it in my heart
when I had thought
it would always
be there to bloom
on spring mornings
by a house, gone
rail and tree
in a town of hintings
and bickering neighbors
whose arguments
were salacious sand
we're immortal here
in this moment!
I had cried
nothing can strip
the bones of our

days but death

came

anyway…

Tara

She doesn't storm
'cause she is bored with sun
she can rain for half a day
and what could be more
natural?

Her wind touches the land
with devastation
fingers the calm
then whispers to a wan
conclusion

That hedges are for gardeners

Nasturtiums for human beings

Passionless Age

To have been born
in such a passionless age
will be my undoing

Thank god for wine
and dream–memory

It's no wonder
that I meter my verse
as I measure my coffee

With a quiet need
especially in the morning

I have become bitter
a fruit too high to pluck
left to fall of its weight

A tree without sweetness
will grow from me soon

***

Still
when I was green
my voice longed to sing
of rage–tender nights!

with hesitant young girls
hiding their under–
developed breasts
behind closed fingers
as Mongol treasures
from marauding hands

Lithe light–creased lips
enfolded in mine
simple
pleasing and profound
was ever feeling like it?
fame nor money
nor power
can compare
to a hesitant kiss
from young love's youth
that tender infancy
of lust's tangled designs

Where the seas of my dreams
soon swelled into being!
new loves now naked
now eager beneath me!

Where brown breasts
heaved warm against my chest
or white and pink as

curved crescent moons
in a mercurial mist
hung down sweetly
shy–offered pears
suspended above me
from a devoted votive
to her incarnate god

Or so I felt
and so I became
both pharaoh and slave
to love's joys and her pains
both and neither
and all and more!

Ah, the gleen
of my young loves' sweat!
heat–slick to the touch
slippery and warm
hair damp–
pressed and matted
pasted against me
as wet sand on my face
while listing her head
on my chest

As the April breezes
soft–sway an acorn

unborn on green grasses

the smell of an oak tree

silent on the wind!

The fertile earth is bed enough

the skies, covers

nakedness no shame

fearless as the stars

unshaken in their course

is my love then!

unshamed and unafraid

And in those bared eyes

bright ovals

I could ponder

the simplest reflections

of love's swift eternities

so green and clear

so brown and clear

so blue and clear

so deep, so frighteningly deep!

I remember them all

So clear

I would wander

within them

lost and alone

only to find myself

not alone

but conjoined

breathing ancient sighs

of amethyst midnight

into those secret delights

and dances of youth!

Sweet youth!

serious, oh so serious youth

and so sweet!

unbridled youth!

bright wild flower!

re–kindle the connection

as lightning the fire

withdrawing like a wave

that good part of myself

left behind

on my lovers' captive shores

Feel for a moment

one eternal moment

Religion, no preacher can preach

Wisdom, no sage can conjure

Belief, no prophet can seer

Grateful for the sweet one
the dear young one!
the hesitant or eager free one!
the one
that brought me both youth
and love and joy...

***

To this day
I've always wanted
to use
more exclamations
in a poem

Many more than were needed
or right or approved
For I didn't – I didn't
when I could feel them
when my life–poetry
demanded them

Since, periods and commas
have done nicely (comma)
thank you (period)

I who've spun rayon
from a distance

watching myself

a stout young Goethe

stride boldly

into love's sorrows and joys

While writing thinly

behind Eliot

his hollowest man

his stuffed man

Who reined in

my passions

when they were red–raw

and ripe

and bit the bit of wit

in my verse

To please an unseen censor

an oh so critical eye

My era

The muses

they are hot blooded beings

Mediterranean

like the ghosts of my past

they have no time

for cold northern lovers

Or

For passionless singers
In a passionless age

Mystic Sand

On the ground of being
ground glass, slippery you
stand unwilling to see the sea
from the land, unable to build
a breakwater in the sand
while breath like muffled sighs
sigh the waves that beat
your feet and legs incessantly
instrumentally cold
as a November gale

My Love of your Morning

My love of your morning
leads me into secret
places of the soul
where your young
lover's eyes are bright
and shining
even as the edge
of a leaf turns yellow
starting to decay
and evening beckons
its deepest mysteries
to unfold
I touch your cheek
awhile
and feel your tears
do you cry for me?
or morning...

Creativity

Circles dance to stillness

ripe with pregnant

names and places

just beyond the fingertips

always ripe like faces

I forgot to remember

ripe like the next

line

and finely final

a breath honed to a

point so sharp

it cuts away sadness

and sorrow and regret

always regret always

till the lines

are seeds and the

earth is wildness

then a pause

to hear the pond

I Have Known Euphoria and Epiphany

I have known euphoria and epiphany

I have dived the depths of friendship

and been broken upon the rocks of betrayal

I have loved with an obsession

to sear the soul

and been torn and shattered

with a life crushing grief

but mostly I have felt the breath

of sorrow

touch my being at times, drop

me to my knees with an ecstasy

that defies words to reach

if after all of this I have gone mad

I accept it

I am sick with living

As the Flower turns to the Sun

As the flower

turns

to the sun

I turn

to the thought

of you

come

I'm brewing tea

by the sea

in each cup

the stars and moon

as the salmon

run

upstream

to be again

I run

to the thought

of you

A Song of Autumn

There is a beauty in the falling leaves
that cling wisp–tight to the buds they were
that reminds me of the sea, the song
that echoes in the seashell

There is a beauty in the drought
that browns the grasses, cracks the earth
with fine lines, fertilizes for future rains
there is a lesson in the fall

There is a beauty in the earth and sea
in erosion and evaporation, that some–
thing so great will become so small
a thing, a moment that glistens in
the dull autumn rain, then releases
on the breezes

I Pour Meaning into the Vessel of my Lives

I pour meaning into the vessel of my lives

new wine in an old bottle

I circumscribe events and tensions

elementary the longings bright like polished glass

look! for the touch of you bending over me

the cut of your absence, the apologies

of tattered dreams

the ache of you tells me that this is my life

new wine in an old bottle

polished glass...

In the end it is only You and I

In the end it is only you and I
after all the trees we loved have been cleared
and the houses filled with raised voices
and silent prayers are gone
when our children who swelling to be born
like beasts of prey have forgotten
their hunting grounds of youth
and the cares of our day
like tired dogs have curled about our feet
to sleep in the golden haze of dreams
will forgetfulness like an anodyne dull our minds
like opiates from some eastern field?
forgotten by the fact, inimitable, that
in the beginning it was only you and I

Silence

Before the noise there was silence
Before the word there was silence
Before the thought there was silence
Before the dream there was silence

After the noise there will be silence
After the word there will be silence
After the thought there will be silence
After the dream there will be silence

I Made Love to my Wife

I made love

to my wife

the night

my mother

died and

as one light

flickered

another burned

I Know Sorrow Now

I know sorrow now though I have called

his name in poetry (often enough)

and prose and worn his face about

the town and posed the unanswerable

question, still we had not met

until today when he called my name

impostor! and slammed shut

the cell, the world gray and vacant

where I must stay and you are gone

I am a Heart

You tell me that injustice's
won and makes justice
apologize for fighting it

You tell me that misery must
be as welcome as summer
tended as spring fields

You tell me I need take ax
to cut out root and branch
burn fields to plant the new crop

But *'I am a heart...*
all I can do is love'

The Song of the Earth and Sea

The sea whispers softly
    'I am that I am'
And the earth responds
    with an earthy glow

Tall the buildings rise
    upon the shoal
Dark the sea winds blow and ride
The dark sea mists of the
    penumbra–ler side

And here we are
    you and I
Somewhere between the stars
    in the sky
And the green–weed
    twisted mysteries
Deep sea–cages
    dark dome–star
Should I go and get the car?

And can we here
And now
And unmoved
Stand

To hear the song of sea and land

    'I am that I am'
    'I am that I am'

Are we?
Can we?!
We can
We can . . .

The city is a silent clash tonight
Riding the many backs
    of sharp steel–dreams
Revolving through the chromium door
    it sleeps no more

Ingrate child
To scorn your parent's lore laid
Bare and unashamed before you
A megalith once ooze and mud
Washed once upon the rocks
You slimed once upon the shore
And have grown
And grown –

Grown cold and colder
Grown old, older
Too old

Too old . . .

'I am that I am'
'I am that I am'

Those children formed
   of clay and foam
Within their mother's
   cavern laid
Within their father's
   silent home
These may hear that hallowed ban
They can
They can . . .

We met amid the chaos
Of (seventh floor/could you hold please)
   creation
And (young boys broken doors)
   destruction
You said,
   Let us go then, you and I, dot, dot, dot
   Like a patient etherized upon a table
And I said,
   That's an old line, dash
   But one of my favorites'

Is *etherized* a word?

And here we still stand

The city's flesh behind us

'Gealing and made whole again

Chit–chatting of this and that

Pondering the mermaid's song

The shore

The sea

A question cornering the corner

    of another's palm

Asking,

    To watch and wait

    Why must it be?

The children seek return –

As the water

    calms

Wraps its fluid arms

Around the soft stone shoal

Which leans

And dissolves

And remains

I wonder –

Should we ever hear

    the song of the earth and sea –

Would we listen?

Would we linger?

Or would we curse and return

To drink social decay

   from a syphilis urn

Gone are the days

Gone are the days of spring–walks and flowers
Gone the times of lake and sky
Gone are the joys of summer's dances
Gone the half–naked joy of coriander and mei

Gone are the fields of golden flowers
Gone the ranges of wheat and tree
Gone are the roaming pasture's linnet
Gone the days of yew and beach

Gone is the wonder in the willow
Gone, all gone, the yellow leaves in fall
Gone are the days of comb and tenet
Gone the dusk that follows all

Cicadas

In a bamboo box a cicada sings for me
its seventeen year song of glory

As the bee–man's beard of bees
the grass moves outside my window
black and brooding

Whispering softly some long gone
memory a melody that was forgotten
when love died in my garden bed

And the cicadas came colored my children's
nightmares, red and black, licorice and blood
how was I to tell them their father had gone away?
when the cicadas came

Curdle Friar

Bent to plumb his dark brown soil
his sun–turned loam, a Mediterranean
memory of olive thighs

The Curdle Friar furrows his toil
his brow knit with subterranean
joys and short staggering sighs

And the smell of sex and Sophia's eyes
afraid and longing, at her small breast
a comb of womb on which his head
might rest, an altar to despise
a silent god, a school–girl's dress

Upon a Wall a Dragon's Claw

Upon a wall a dragon's claw
offers up a wedding sword
beneath the epitaph of Shakespeare

Good friend for Iesus sake forbeare,
To digg the dvst encloased heare.
Blese be ye man yt spares thes stones.
And cvrst be he yt moves my bones.

A sword of thought
that cuts truth from lie
can one live by another's
dying wish?

Outside the others rush to work
the dawn on another day of gain
and I, a moron, a buffoon sit
questioning if there is a beauty
that can survive ugliness

Ah, who will fight for this lost bay
a dying tree, leaves brown and moldy?

Yeats went forward and found his comfort
in a daughter plea that she not be too pretty

an alloy want that steel and fire made pure

Keat's carried an opposing fire

Beauty is truth, truth beauty, – that is all

Ye know on earth, and all ye need to know.

Upon a wall a dragon's claw

offers up a wedding sword

above the romances of Mallory

the laughing Buddha

and the owl with the crooked eye

Curving Pendulous

Curving pendulous arching upward to a flower, a heart

–pink pastiche nature's source and nourishment abound

–ing round and full–dimpled dappled point d'appui

a porringer of comfort and solace, warmth and sustenance

a baby's pacifier, a boy's release, an old man's pillow

budding in the seed, a grape full sweet on the vine

a raisin forgotten as sun–fallow the curves straighten

to fertilize a memory of hunger and hope, desire and need

A Goth's Arch

A Goth's arch holding back a nihilist's world, perhaps
some green paint flaking at the edge, solder aging cracking
framing, holding together a picture painted of light and glass
and a dark–skinned child, more energy than mass, more eyes
than tongue, more hope than fear, who looking up wonders why
the gold–haired boy and girl kneel to the tall man with light for
a head, his hand out–stretched to touch their brow patiently, unlike
a father would when watching TV, or walking out the door.

Naked as the Sunshine

Naked as the sunshine, soft sand cradling a wet wave

time's hand tiding out a teeny pink suit with silver frill, as

she squeals and flings a chubby finger, points to the horizon

her bottom white with sand and salt and smooth and

bare as an eternity masquerading as a moment–tarry missive

a prayer to a round venus figurine in a polka–dot frock

stretched close to catch the sprite sheening joy without care

horrified what the onlookers, the saprophytes might think.

Red Clover Grows

Red clover grows like unwashed blood
on the field of honor, as memory wisps through
sparse green grasses o'er the grassy knoll, a tribute
to blue truth like selentine sky and gray passion
churling dark and noble on the horizon of a day
and time, a hope and dream, an ache and assassination

We Read to Know
(we're not alone)

If these words could talk
they'd tell you we've done this
before but if it will comfort you
we'll wind back again:

To a salutary time
a softer fire
cascading to caress
your colder heart
to press its melancholy sweetness
for the vintner
for your fire now flickers
now cycles–round
wired plastic boxes
tethered to other
wired plastic boxes
yet you seek warmth waiting
watching to feel alone

Morning and evening
maids heard the goblins cry

If these words could talk
they would sing a song

of Zion and damask'd honey

of rose and twisted thorn

they would flay you

for a touch of the belovèd

ache inside you like heartbreak

sing inside you their dark songs

Why beauty flown?

why steel and stone?

If these words could talk

they would decimate you

surge truths, etch the edges

of your copper life

corrode the contacts of your silicon

fantasies, more emptied than

the sediments of sentiments

grown sweet and decaying

whispered and cloyed

Vitae summa brevis spem

nos vetat incohare longam[1]

If these words could talk

they *would* talk to tell you

---

1 - "The brief sum of life forbids us cling to far-off hope." - Horace

of the desolateness of pixels dancing

before dead eyes, Mississippi ghosts

burning

terra–rime romances grown silent

and dismayed

Will I Live Another Day?

Will I live another day? who's to say
I've seen the sun shimmer the water
at sunrise and savored the kisses
of a young love new born
and been lost and sad
as a sand piper's cry
on a beach long eroded
I've tasted cold water
on a hot summer's day
and been glad

Will I live one more day? it may be
to see the moon whiten the oak trees
at midnight or smell the green scent
of April's return
I've been happy, at peace

I've shared the love
of ripened arms and seen
the birth of my children
giving thanks for their lives
for their life's sake only
knowing some of the things
that they must face

Will I live another day? I don't know –

but I have lived today

Made in United States
Orlando, FL
22 March 2026

79568232R00036